BUSES OF WESTERN FLYER and NEW FLYER INDUSTRIES
PHOTO ARCHIVE

William A. Luke and Linda L. Metler

Iconografix

Iconografix
PO Box 446
Hudson, Wisconsin 54016 USA

Library of Congress Control Number: 2008944045

ISBN-13: 978-1-58388-229-0
ISBN-10: 1-58388-229-4

09 10 11 12 13 14 6 5 4 3 2 1

Printed in China

Cover and book design by Dan Perry

Copyediting by Andy Lindberg

COVER: The Lane Transit District, Eugene, Oregon, began a Bus Rapid Transit (BRT) service betwen Eugene and neighboring Springfield in January 2007. It was branded as the EMX service. Pictured is one of the New Flyer diesel electric articulated buses that were chosen to operate on the BRT route. An exclusive roadway over much of the route is featured. The EMX buses also operate over short sections of city streets. Additional pictures of the buses on the BRT route can be seen on page 80.

BOOK PROPOSALS

Iconografix is a publishing company specializing in books for transportation enthusiasts. We publish in a number of different areas, including Automobiles, Auto Racing, Buses, Construction Equipment, Emergency Equipment, Farming Equipment, Railroads & Trucks. The Iconografix imprint is constantly growing and expanding into new subject areas.

Authors, editors, and knowledgeable enthusiasts in the field of transportation history are invited to contact the Editorial Department at Iconografix, Inc., PO Box 446, Hudson, WI 54016.

www.iconografixinc.com

TABLE OF CONTENTS

ACKNOWLEDGEMENTS

New Flyer Industries, Winnipeg, Manitoba
Alex Regiec, president, Manitoba Transit Heritage Association, Winnipeg, Manitoba
Paul Leger, president, Bus History Association, Halifax, Nova Scotia
Paul Bateson, bus historian, Brampton, Ontario
Bill and Lucy MacDonald, Vancouver, British Columbia

BIBLIOGRAPHY

Motor Coach Age, September 1984
Bus Ride Magazine, various issues, 1965-1996
Dusty Trails to Divided Highways, by Alex Regiec, Dennis Cavanaugh, and David Anthony Wyatt
Coachways Equipment-History, by Brian E. Sullivan
Various newspaper articles, sales literature and other publications

FOREWORD

We were very pleased to hear that William Luke was crafting a book depicting the rich history of New Flyer. Bill is widely considered the foremost authority in the world on bus history and an old and dear friend of New Flyer. He has personally known every president and CEO of the company and is a gracious and generous source of information for the whole industry. It is an honor to write this foreword and add our perspective to this pictorial journey through our history.

When Western Auto and Truck Body Works Company was founded in 1930, John Coval brought with him significant experience in the design and manufacture of transportation vehicles. He also brought an understanding that in order to be successful in this very competitive industry, especially in the heart of the Canadian prairies, a company must provide the absolute best product and service, period.

Even in the '30s and '40s, it was clear that diversity and innovation were necessary for the company to thrive. In addition to the inter-city bus market, WATBW introduced a new kind of camping trailer, stretch sedan style buses, tour buses, and semi-trailer vans—whatever it took to satisfy the customer's needs.

Through creative thinking and listening to the requirements and desires of customers, in 1945 the company created a defining and prophetic vehicle—the "Western Flyer" coach. This vehicle became the focus and ultimately the namesake of the company. As Mr. Coval put it, "This was a unit so designed and constructed as to combat and withstand the terrain and the climatic conditions that existed in our field of operation."

The "Western Flyer Canuck" built in 1953 was an example of how important it is to listen to your customers. The early versions of this bus model, which were developed to compete with other organizations that were offering a similar vehicle, were not well accepted. After several redesigns based on customer feedback, the Canuck finally became the bus the customers wanted, and this design became the foundation for the company, and the benchmark for the industry. The success of this model marked a turning point in the company's history. For the first time, the company focused on innovative and reliable products for the transit industry.

Years of numerous and significant ownership/management changes contributed to a quieter period in our history, but when Jan den Oudsten acquired the company in 1986, he brought new European designs and technology to address the needs of North American transit customers. The company experienced a rebirth, slowly and methodically returning to the position of industry leader with its new name, New Flyer, and with an innovative and diverse product line. Technology advancements introduced by New Flyer during this era (such as low-floor designs for accessibility, the programmable logic control multiplexing system for reduced complexity and the 60-foot articulating vehicle to accommodate higher passenger volumes) have remained the North American industry standard.

Now, at the time this book is being produced, we are on the cusp of delivering the first of 20 hydrogen hybrid buses to BC Transit—the first hydrogen fleet in the world—which will be showcased at the 2010 Winter Olympics in Vancouver, BC, Canada. The vehicles will operate with zero emissions and a completely renewable fuel source.

Different regions have unique requirements for their transit systems ranging from basic urban transit service to Bus Rapid Transit. On the international stage, public transit is seen increasingly as the solution to pollution, rising fuel costs, energy conservation and traffic congestion. This has led to our current, industry-leading offering of hybrid buses, compressed and liquefied natural gas buses, clean diesel buses, fuel cell buses and electrified trolley buses in a number of different configurations in lengths of 30 to 60 feet. And, as our customers' needs evolve, we will continue to innovate and adapt.

As you read through this book and witness the evolution of our company and its products, keep in mind that one thing has remained constant through New Flyer's long history. The driving force behind the advancements and the success of the company was always, ultimately, our customers.

That is the one thing that will never change at New Flyer.

John Marinucci
President and CEO
New Flyer Industries

WESTERN FLYER/NEW FLYER INTRODUCTION

Western Flyer Auto & Truck Body Works began producing buses in 1930. Adapting to changes in the bus industry, taking advantage of opportunities, and being interested in serving was the direction in the early days. This formula continues today with New Flyer Industries.

John Coval, the founder of Western Auto & Truck Body Works, incorporated the company in 1931. He had emigrated from the Ukraine and settled in Winnipeg, Manitoba. He began working for the Standard Carriage Co., which specialized in vehicle body building. Truck body installation was the emphasis and the bodies were built to the customers' needs. While at Standard Carriage Company, John helped build bus bodies for many of the early bus operators in the area.

Canadian bus companies were experiencing the necessity of having vehicles specialized for passenger service that was safe, dependable, and comfortable in the Canadian environment. Highways were expanding and remote areas were destinations. Bus companies were expanding their routes. Harsh winter weather conditions created another challenge to the bus operators as well as Western Auto & Truck Body Works. Buses had to be built to adapt to the conditions. John Coval recognized this and built the buses at his factory to adapt to the rough gravel roads and the extreme winter temperatures. At first the buses were built on truck chassis, but more integral construction followed, with a strong frame and body. The Western buses were attractive looking and offered comfort to passengers on long trips. Because it was difficult to find sturdy seats from manufacturers, Western built its own bus seats, comfortable, but sturdy.

A building at 702 Broadway near downtown Winnipeg was where the Western Auto & Truck Body Works bus construction took place. It was not a large facility, but it was able to take on the demand, at the time, for buses. There was a certain standardization to even the earliest buses built, although buses could be customized easily to meet the customers requirements.

Western Flyer became the name given the buses in 1941 and the new name was an effective marketing move. Western Flyer buses were operating throughout Canada, especially in Manitoba. Grey Goose Bus Line was one of the important Winnipeg area customers. Red River Motor Coach Lines (also of Winnipeg) was another, followed by Manitoba Motor Transit, Ltd. of Brandon, Manitoba.

During the early days of Western Auto & Truck Body Works, tourism was taking on importance, especially in the national parks of the Canadian Rockies. Railroads were bringing many tourists to the parks. Roads, mostly gravel, were built to many scenic locations. Sightseeing companies and tourist hotels had been using motorized vehicles to give the advantage of seeing the magnificent scenery. John Coval was in close contact with the sightseeing companies and in 1937 Western built open-top bodies on Ford chassis for Brewster Transport, a large sightseeing company in Banff, Alberta. In 1940 glass top sightseeing bodies were built for Brewster on Ford and Dodge chassis to update the company's fleet and also allow for all weather sightseeing. Two similar plexi-glass top sightseeing buses were built for the Salt Lake (Utah) Transportation Co. They were believed to be the first Canadian-built buses sold in the United States.

During World War II, Western Auto & Truck Body Works temporarily stopped bus building. The company did build 12,000 truck bodies for the Canadian Ministries and Supply Department including 600 truck bodies for the United National Relief and Rehabilitation Administration (UNRRA).

Following World War II, it was back to bus building. The standard type bus, the T-28, and a new T-32 model were in demand. The Manitoba customers were expanding and adding buses and new bus companies were recognizing the Western-built buses. New roads to remote regions were opening and new bus services were inaugurated. Canadian Coachways, an Alberta company, was expanding very rapidly and Western Flyer buses were proving to be the most suitable bus. Saskatchewan Transportation Company was established in 1946 and became a good Western Flyer customer. The name of the company was changed to Western Flyer Coach, Ltd. in 1945 reflecting the popularity of the name.

John Coval saw more potential for Western Flyer coaches and established a number of customers in Quebec province. He traveled to Quebec and although he could not speak French, the French-speaking Quebec bus people liked John and liked Western Flyer buses. Southern Ontario also proved to be a good market.

Although engine choices were up to the customer, most post-war Western Flyer buses came with International Red Diamond 450-horsepower gasoline engines. Some style changes were made, particularly longer side windows. There were also three deck-and-a-half models built reflecting the customizing that Western was able to perform. Larger buses were also introduced, the T-36/40 models accommodating up to 40 passengers.

Highways throughout Canada were improving and more modern buses with rear engines and more modern styling were desired. In 1953 Western Flyer Coach introduced its first rear-engined bus which was called the "Canuck," a slang term for Canadian. A prototype 33-passenger bus was built, and refined two years later with a larger higher version and designated as the P-37 Canuck. A 41 Canuck followed later. Almost all Canucks had diesel engines, mainly Detroit Diesel 6-71 or 6-V71, although some had the smaller Detroit Diesel 4-71 diesel engine. Some like the prototype were powered by Cummins diesel engines. In building the Canuck models, Western Flyer people knew the buses would still see service on dusty, gravel roads. Therefore, the engine, radiator and other units were fully enclosed, but with an air intake on the roof at the rear. The new Canuck model was successful and almost 600 were built between 1955 and 1966.

Canadian Coachways was expanding services throughout the North. The Western Flyer Standard front-engined buses, which had been in operation for several years traveling mainly on gravel roads, were extremely reliable. They also had to tolerate temperatures to -40 degrees for extended periods. When the rear-engined Canuck models were produced, there was concern whether they would be able to perform as well. They did and some covered over a million miles, almost entirely on gravel roads and at extremely low temperatures in the winters. These buses also received high praise by the bus companies which had them in their fleets.

During the 1960s, John Coval sold Western Flyer Coach to Abraham Thiessen and his associates. Thiessen headed Grey Goose Bus Lines, which had originated from the early 1920s under another ownership. A new name, Western Flyer Coach (1964), became the reorganized name. The first major change was a new factory built in the Fort Garry Industrial

Park in Winnipeg. It was a modern building capable of increased production.

In the late 1960s it was decided to discontinue building highway buses and begin producing city buses. A prototype forty-foot transit bus, the Model 700, was produced and went into tests on Winnipeg Transit services. Later it was acquired by Winnipeg Transit. More than 300 Model 700 buses were built.

Soon afterward an opportunity came to bid on the construction of bodies for 151 trolley buses for the Toronto Transit Commission to replace an aging trolley bus fleet. The bid was accepted, and the bodies were completed. Electric motors for the trolley buses were refurbished motors from older trolley buses. Flyer Industries also built bodies for 40 trolley buses for the Hamilton (Ontario) Street Railway. They also had refurbished electric motors.

The Thiessen involvement in the bus building ended in 1971. The Manitoba Development Corporation acquired the company at that time and Flyer Industries, Ltd. became the new name.

Two years later, Flyer Industries introduced the 800 series transit buses and trolley buses. Between 1973 and 1978, 580 Model 800 diesel buses and 558 Model 800 trolley buses were built by Flyer Industries in a new site in Transcona, a suburban and industrial area east of Winnipeg.

Flyer Industries continued to play an active role in the manufacture of trolley buses, even though most cities in the United States and Canada had discontinued operating trolley buses ten to twenty years before. San Francisco Municipal Railway with a large fleet of trolley buses began a fleet renewal in 1976 and an order was placed with Flyer Industries for 343 E800 trolley buses. This was the second largest order for trolley buses ever in the United States. Vancouver, British Columbia, also replaced its trolley bus fleet placing an order in 1975 for 50 units and in 1982 for 300.

Boston, Massachusetts, and Dayton, Ohio, also renewed their trolley bus fleets with Flyer Industries E800 models in 1976.

The 900 series Flyer Industries model entered the transit bus market in 1978. It was possible to sell the buses in the United States and Chicago, Illinois, Seattle, Washington, Oakland, California, and other cities bought the new model.

In 1986, Jan den Oudsten, who had been associated with the pioneer Dutch bus building firm Den Oudsten Bussen NV, purchased Flyer Industries. Because of the new ownership, the name of the company was changed to New Flyer Industries.

Production of articulated buses began in 1988 with model D60HF. The first articulated buses went into service in Vancouver, British Columbia. AC Transit in Oakland, California, was another early bus system to acquire the D60HF model.

With the new ownership and some of the expertise from Europe, New Flyer Industries designed, tested, and introduced the first low-floor bus in North America. The 40-foot low-floor bus went into initial service for the Port Authority of New York and New Jersey in 1988. Shuttle service was operated by that organization in the area. After a trial, 40 of the New Flyer low-floor buses were purchased by the Port Authority of New York and New Jersey after full production of the model began in 1991.

Transit in Vancouver, British Columbia, was the first transit system to order the New Flyer Model D40LF low-floor buses and ten went into service. St. Albert (Alberta), Las Vegas, Chicago and Phoenix were some of the cities with the first D40LF buses.

Programmable Logic Controlled (PLC) Multiplexing was introduced and was standard on all New Flyer buses after 1993. This was an significant innovation, which gave important maintenance diagnoses and eliminated considerable wiring.

Expanding production by New Flyer Industries resulted in adding additional production facilities. The first one was in Grand Forks, North Dakota, in 1990 and six years later it was moved to Crookston, Minnesota. In 1999 a state-of-the-art production facility opened in St. Cloud, Minnesota. It is 338,000 square feet and almost as large as the main factory in Winnipeg. The Crookston facility is 68,000 square feet.

Another significant trolley bus the E60HF was produced by New Flyer. Sixty went into service for the San Francisco Municipal Railway in 1994.

In 1998, the first 60-foot articulated low-floor buses were introduced. Two Washington State transit systems, Community Transit of Snohomish County and King County Metro of Seattle placed the first orders. Community Transit received ten of the new D60LF buses and King County Metro began operating 100 D60LF New Flyer buses.

In the 1990s, New Flyer Industries began delivering alternate fueled transit buses. San Diego Transit and other California cities acquired a number of compressed natural gas fuelled buses. Liquefied natural gas powered buses were also produced. Diesel electric hybrid and even gasoline electric were tested early by New Flyer and deliveries began after 2000.

Harvest Partners & Lightyear Capital bought New Flyer Industries in 2004. Jan de Oudsten retired. For his outstanding achievements he was inducted in the American Public Transportation Association Hall of Fame in 2002. John Marinucci became the new president and CEO of New Flyer Industries.

New Flyer Industries had been developing diesel electric hybrid buses for several years. Production began in 2004 and King County Metro of Seattle ordered 213 of the hybrid buses, Model DE60LF. New Flyer received numerous orders for hybrid buses following the initial introduction.

Hydrogen fuel cell propulsion received early testing by New Flyer Industries and the first fleet of 20 New Flyer hydrogen fuel cell buses will go into service later this year by BC Transit for service in Whistler, British Columbia, the site for the 2010 Winter Olympics. It is an important introduction because the new buses will be showcased to the world.

In 2004, New Flyer Industries began delivering a new styled trolley bus. The first of 188 Model E40LF low-floor trolley buses began service in Vancouver, British Columbia, for the Coast Mountain Bus Company in 2005. The new trolley buses were followed by 40 Model E60LF articulated low floor trolley buses which entered service in 2007. The Southeastern Pennsylvania Transit Authority in Philadelphia, Pennsylvania, also has a fleet of New Flyer E40LF trolley buses replacing older vehicles. Philadelphia is one of the oldest continually operating trolley bus systems in the world, beginning in 1923.

Another special design New Flyer articulated bus, the BRT60LF, entered service for an award winning Bus Rapid Transit service in Eugene, Oregon. The system operates mostly on its own roadway and has doors on both sides to facilitate Bus Rapid Transit stations in order for one station to serve the vehicles going in either direction. Similar New Flyer BRT articulateds entered service on the Silver Line Bus Rapid Transit route on Cleveland, Ohio's Euclid Avenue. Although the Eugene and Cleveland buses are special Bus Rapid Transit vehicles, these New Flyer buses are not new to Bus Rapid Transit services because they have been in service on Bus

Rapid Transit busways in Ottawa, Ontario and Pittsburgh, Pennsylvania, for a number of years.

Western Flyer had an interesting and unique history which was highlighted by the fact that the company knew its customers and helped them pioneer their services in Canada. Today, as New Flyer Industries is reaching its 80th anniversary, the company is building advanced technology buses that are environmentally friendly, relieving congestion and helping to improve communities everywhere.

Jan den Oudsten

John Coval

John Coval worked at the Standard Carriage Company in Winnipeg, Manitoba, before he founded Western Auto & Truck Body Works in 1930. While at Standard Carriage, he worked on bus body construction learning the trade. One of the buses that came from Standard Carriage was this one built on a Chevrolet truck chassis. It was built for Beacon Bus Line, a small, short-lived bus line in the Winnipeg area.

This view shows the Western Auto & Truck Body Works Broadway plant in 1935 with buses in the process of being built. John Coval with the dark suit and cigar is showing plans to a plant supervisor. *Photo Gar Peverley – Paul Leger Collection*

Pictured is a bus being constructed on a Maple Leaf chassis in the Western Auto & Truck Body Works factory in Winnipeg, Manitoba, in the mid-1930s. *Photo Gar Peverley – Paul Leger Collection*

Shown in these two pictures is a Checker Greyhound Lines of Regina, Saskatchewan bus that was rebodied by the Western Auto & Truck Body Works in 1935. The bus was originally a Yellow Coach Model V and had 50,000 miles (80,000 km) before it was rebodied. *Photos Gar Peverley – Paul Leger Collection*

This Western Auto and Truck Body Works T-28 bus was acquired by Clark Transportation Company Ltd. in 1940. Clark originally had two routes from Winnipeg, one to Neepawa and Dauphin and one to Brandon. The Brandon route was transferred to Manitoba Motor Transit Company in 1933. Eleven years later, after the Dauphin route had been extended to Yorkton, Saskatchewan, Clark Transportation Company went out of business, selling to Western Canadian Greyhound Lines.

Western Auto & Truck Body Works in Winnipeg, Manitoba, built this T-28 Model bus for B.C. Greyhound Lines of Penticton, British Columbia, in 1941. It was built on a Kenworth chassis and had a Buda L-0525 gasoline engine. B.C. Greyhound began in 1935 and operated routes in southern British Columbia serving Princeton, Penticton, Vernon and Trail. The company was acquired by Central Canadian Greyhound Lines in 1944.

Arrow Coach Lines of Saskatoon, Saskatchewan, acquired this early 28-passenger bus in 1940 from Western Auto & Truck Body Works in Winnipeg. Arrow Coach Lines began in 1931 and operated several routes in Saskatchewan serving Yorkton, Regina, Moose Jaw and Prince Albert. An international route entered the United States and terminated in Glendive, Montana. In 1934, another Saskatchewan bus company, Gray Line Motor Stages, merged with Arrow Coach Lines. Arrow Coach Lines, including Gray Line Motor Stages, was sold to Central Canadian Greyhound Lines.

Three Manitoba Motor Transit pre-World War II, 28-passenger buses built by Western Auto & Truck Body Works in Winnipeg are shown at the bus station in Brandon, headquarters of the company. Manitoba Motor Transit Company began in 1929 as the Northern Manitoba Bus Company. The name was changed in 1933.

In 1940, Western Auto & Truck Body Works built the body for this bus on a British Leyland Diesel chassis. It was the first diesel bus to come from the Western plant. International Transit, Ltd. supplied the chassis. After the body was added the company operated the bus on its routes in the Port Arthur-Fort William (now Thunder Bay), Ontario, area.

Western Auto & Truck Body Works, Ltd. was involved in converting passenger automobiles into larger capacity vehicles. Pictured is a 1940 LaSalle which was lengthened and the roof removed to allow for sightseeing by passengers. This vehicle was purchased by Jasper Park Lodge in Alberta for sightseeing and rail transfers.

This 1941 Ford truck chassis had a sedan-type body built by Western Auto & Truck Body Works. At the time, Western was building sightseeing vehicles for national parks in Alberta and other areas. The owner of this unusual vehicle is not known and it may only have been a demonstrator.

In 1937, Brewster Transport, Banff, Alberta, had Western Auto & Truck Body Works in Winnipeg, Manitoba, mount sightseeing bus bodies on two 1937 Ford truck chassis. These buses operated sightseeing service to the many Banff National Park area scenic attractions. They joined a fleet of much older vehicles.

Western Auto and Truck Body Works, Ltd. built nine bus bodies on Ford and Dodge truck chassis in 1946 for Brewster Transport in Banff, Alberta. The pioneer sightseeing company was preparing for an influx of tourists following World War II and the company's sightseeing bus fleet needed updating. These buses are pictured at the Columbia Icefields. They had plexiglass roofs to allow passengers unlimited viewing in all weather conditions.

At one time Canadian Coachways was one of the largest bus systems in Canada. It began in 1929 with a 100-mile route from Edmonton, Alberta, to Athabaska. As the roads north of Edmonton expanded, so did Coachways. Pictured is one of the first Western Flyer buses purchased by Canadian Coachways. It was a 1944 Model T-28 Standard bus, one of four in the Coachways fleet.

This Model T-32 bus, built by Western Auto & Truck Body Works, was bought by Northland Arrow Lines of Edmonton, Alberta, about 1945. One of the design changes to this bus was the oval side windows. Northland Arrow Lines operated its main routes from Edmonton to Barrhead and Fort Assinibone. The company was associated with the Edmonton-based Sunburst Lines, Ltd. Both companies were acquired by Canadian Coachways in 1966.

In 1946, the province of Saskatchewan nationalized bus service. In doing so the new company, Saskatchewan Transportation Company (STC), took over all the bus services in the province except the interprovincial services of Western Canadian Greyhound Line. Among the first STC buses were 25 Western Flyer T-28 and T-32 models. An STC T-32 is pictured. Ten more similar models were added in the following years. Most were powered by International 450-horsepower gasoline engines, but a few had White engines.

Western Auto & Truck Body Works built buses in this building at 702 Broadway in Winnipeg, Manitoba, from the 1940s until 1964. About half of the 135 employees are pictured in front of the building and a Model T-36 bus. A smaller building on Portage Avenue in Winnipeg was also used.

Western Auto & Truck Body Works had the ability to build buses of different sizes and also build for customers with special needs. This small-sized Model T-21 bus was built for International Transit, Ltd. of Port Arthur (now Thunder Bay), Ontario, in 1947. It had a Hercules engine. International Transit was a pioneer company. In the 1920s it operated between Port Arthur and Duluth, Minnesota. Later that route was cut back to the U.S.-Canadian border where it connected with Greyhound Lines.

Northern Bus Lines, Flin Flon, Manitoba, had its beginnings as Lake View Bus in the late 1930s. About ten years later the name Northern Bus Lines, Ltd. was established. The company operated school buses and town bus service in Flin Flon. The only two-door, city-type bus built by Western Flyer Coach was acquired by Northern Bus Lines in 1950 for town service. In 1952 Northern Bus Lines became a wholly owned subsidiary of the Winnipeg-based Beaver Bus Lines. The Hudson Bay Mining and Smelter Company contracted with Northern to carry workers to their facilities. Northern is now under a new owner and provides all the bus service in the area.

This Western Flyer Model T-32, built in 1948, was purchased by the British Yukon Navigation Company (BYN) headquartered in Seattle, Washington. The bus was based in Whitehorse, Yukon Territory. BYN began bus service October 7, 1945, replacing the Northwest Service Command Bus Service. By April 1, 1946, BYN was operating the bus over the famous Alaska Highway between Whitehorse and Dawson Creek, British Columbia. In 1956, Canadian Coachways took over the BYN service. BYN also had a 1950 Model T-32 Western Flyer and a 1947 Model T-23 Western Flyer with a Ford G6 engine. International 450-horsepower engines were in the other BYN Western Flyer buses.

Canadian National Transportation, Ltd. was incorporated March 19, 1931, to operate all highway routes of the Canadian National Railways Co. Pictured is one of the three Model T-34/40 Western Flyer buses purchased in 1953. They all had International 450-horsepower gasoline engines. The buses were first operated between Kamsack, Saskatchewan, and Flin Flon, Manitoba. The service ended in 1985 and the buses were transferred to the Canadian National Transportation Services in St. Catharines, Ontario, for service in that area.

More than half of the total number of buses built by Western Auto & Truck Body Works and Western Flyer Coach were buses for various government agencies such as the Canadian Department of National Defense consisting of the Army, Navy and Air Force. A total of 367 government buses were built between 1949 and 1965. These buses were mainly T-40 and C-40 models with some custom variations. International 450-horsepower Red Diamond gasoline engines were the primary engines used, but Buda, Dodge and Ford engines powered some of the buses. A few were built as conventional models on Dodge chassis with the engine out in front. The U.S. Air Force had a special C-28 model with four-wheel drive. The Royal Canadian Air Force also had four-wheel-drive Western Flyer buses. These buses presumably were used at remote outposts for travel on unimproved and snowy roads.

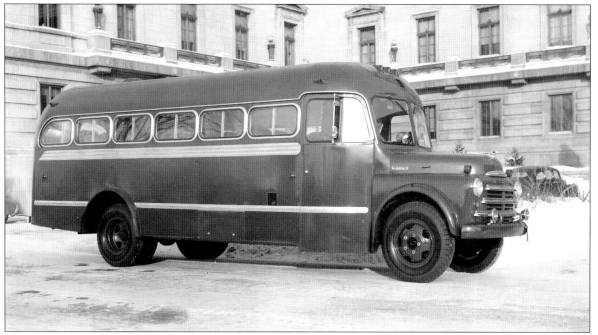

Three of these Dodge conventional buses were built for the Canadian Department of National Defense in 1950. These buses were the only ones known to be built by Western Flyer Coach in the 1950s on full chassis with the engine in front and outside the body. This type of bus demonstrated the custom bus-building capabilities of the company.

Western Flyer Coach built this special Model C-28 bus for the U. S. Air Force. It was a four-wheel-drive vehicle supposedly to be used at a far north air base which would experience considerable snow. The bus was able to serve the base under harsh weather conditions. An International 305-horsepower Blue Diamond engine powered the bus. The U.S. Air Force bought three other Western Flyer standard buses, but only one with four-wheel drive.

The Royal Canadian Air Force Training Command Band was one of the Air Force units that had a Western Flyer Model T-40 bus. Most of the buses of the Department of National Defense were painted an overall dark color, probably an olive or brown. However, this bus for the band sported a more attractive livery.

This Western Flyer T-40 Standard model was delivered to Beaver Bus Lines, Ltd. in early 1949. It had 40 non-reclining seats. Beaver Bus Lines originated in 1939, although its routes go back to 1932. In 1948, when Winnipeg Electric Company discontinued an intercity route between Winnipeg and Selkirk, Beaver acquired the route. John Fehr, Sr. became the owner of Beaver Bus Lines in 1972, and it continues to be a family bus business today.

Grey Goose Bus Lines, Ltd. was one of the pioneer bus companies in Manitoba. It had its beginnings in 1924, but the name was not registered until ten years later. The company operated some of the first buses built by Western Auto & Truck Body Works, including this T-32/40 Standard bus of 1950. Grey Goose Bus Lines operated many Western-built buses.

Interlake Bus Lines, Ltd. got its name because its routes served an area north of Winnipeg between Lake Winnipeg and Lake Manitoba. It began in 1936 and 15 years later the company was sold to Grey Goose Bus Lines. Like many Manitoba bus operators, Interlake chose Western Flyer buses. Pictured is one of the Model T-32/36 models added in 1951.

Although Red River Motor Coach Lines, Ltd. had several bus types, it was a good customer for Western Flyer buses. It had four Western Flyer T-32 or T-36/40 models. Pictured is one of the T-32 Western Flyer buses which entered service for Red River in 1948. Appropriately the buses were painted red and white. The company was sold in 1962 to Grey Goose Bus Lines.

Western Flyer Coach introduced the Western Flyer Junior in 1954. It had 28 reclining seats and a 186-inch wheelbase. An International 305-horsepower engine was used. Long side windows along with glass windows on the roof were featured. The Canadian National Railways bought this Western Flyer Junior for its Jasper Park Lodge in Alberta.

Services Inter Citie (Intercity Bus Line) of Saint-Hyacinthe, Quebec, purchased this Model T-32/36 Western Flyer in 1951. Services Inter Citie was a good customer of Western Flyer. Two more T-32/36 buses and a T-36/40 followed for the Inter Citie fleet. A Model P-41 Western Canuck was purchased in 1959. Services Inter Citie reportedly began in the 1930s and mainly served the Saint-Hyacinthe, Granby, Iberville and Saint-Jean areas. New owners bought the company in 1948, and in 1975 the company was sold to Verreault Transport Ltd.

Manitoba Motor Transport. Ltd. of Brandon, Manitoba, bought four Standard buses from Western Flyer in the late 1940s and early 1950s. Pictured is one of the T-36/40 models acquired in 1953. Like most of the Western Flyer buses of that time it had an International Red Diamond 450-horsepower gasoline engine.

Asbestos Transit, Inc. had its beginning in 1945, operating from its base in Victoriaville, Quebec. It served a route between Victoriaville and Asbestos to Ste-Angele. This Western Flyer Model T-32 was the only Western Flyer bus acquired new by Asbestos Transit, although a Junior 35 model Western Flyer, originally owned by Autobus R Michel, was added to the fleet later.

In 1954, the Western Flyer T-36 had a styling change. Thiessen Transportation, Ltd. bought one of the first models which featured longer and higher side windows. Thiessen Transportation Ltd. began in 1946 and had two routes from Winnipeg, one to Winkler and one to Gretna. Under the leadership of Abraham Thiessen the company bought a number of Winnipeg area bus lines including Grey Goose Bus Lines. Grey Goose Bus Lines was the name adopted for the entire Thiessen system. Western Flyer Coach was purchased by Thiessen in 1963.

In 1954, Red Cliff Bus Company of Red Cliff, Alberta, was one of the first companies to add this newly styled Western Flyer Model T36/40 bus to its fleet. The company operated a short route between Red Cliff and Medicine Hat, a distance of eight kilometers (five miles). Later Red Cliff bought two Western Canuck Model P-41 buses and used them primarily for charter service. The company originated as a taxi company in 1932 and was discontinued in the mid-1980s.

One of several Quebec bus companies which operated Western Flyer buses was Montmorency Transport Company of Quebec City. It operated a suburban route between Quebec City and Ste-Anne de Beaupre. The service was known as Autobus Eugene Dupont, Engr. when it began in 1937. The Montmorency name was adopted in 1948. The Western Flyer Model T-36/40 with long side windows was the first Western Flyer acquired by Montmorency. Two used Western Flyer buses were later added to the fleet. The scheduled route was discontinued in late 1988, and charter and sightseeing service became the main focus. Dupont Tours now operates the company.

This Model T-32/36 Western Flyer was sold to a Quebec company, Autobus Ste-Claire Ste-Justine St-Narcisse Ltee. in 1956. It was built when rear-engined Model P-37 Western Flyers were in production and front-engined models were being phased out for bus companies by Western Flyer Coach. Autobus Ste-Claire Ste-Justine Ste-Narcisse Ltee. was a small, little known bus company, but it had a surprisingly rich history dating back to 1922. There were several owners of the company prior to the adoption of the long company name in 1945. Several route extensions were made to small villages east of Quebec City. The route continued until late in the 1990s, but was ended because of the lack of patronage.

The prototype rear-engined Western Flyer Coach called the Canuck was introduced in 1954. It had 33 reclining seats and a Cummins JB 8000 gasoline engine at first, but it was later replaced with an International Red Diamond gasoline engine. The coach had small wide windows, but later production models had larger side windows. Moore's Taxi, Ltd. started as a large taxi company in Winnipeg in the 1920s, but it was not until much later that it began operating the Winnipeg–Kenora, Ontario, route. It used the name Moore's Trans-Canada Bus Line. Moore's also operated the first P-37/41 Canuck model. Because Moore's buses on the Kenora route were in Winnipeg daily, Western Flyer people were able to observe each new model closely.

Moose Mountain Lines, Ltd., Regina, Saskatchewan, was established in 1955 and had a single route between Regina and Wawota, Saskatchewan, on Highway 16. After a new owner, Alex Bishop, acquired the company, it expanded, adding two more routes and obtaining extensive charter authority. In 1955, the company purchased this P 37-41 Western Flyer Canuck, one of the first of this model built. It had a Cummins JB 800D rear engine. Another Canuck P-41 was added in 1960.

WESTERN FLYER COACH LIMITED
WINNIPEG - MANITOBA

Pictured is the first Western Flyer P-39 bus purchased by Saskatchewan Transportation Company (STC) of Regina, Saskatchewan. STC bought 21 Model P-37s and the larger P-41s from Western Flyer Coach, Limited between 1956 and 1962. More than 100 of these models were built, and STC had the largest fleet of these two buses. The first P-37 models had GM 4-71 diesel engines while the P-41 Models had GM 6V-71 diesel engines.

This Western Flyer Model P-41R Canuck was the only Western Flyer to be in the Greyhound Lines of Canada fleet. It was originally ordered by Moore's Trans Canada Bus Lines but was still in production when Moore's sold its Winnipeg-Kenora route to Greyhound Lines of Canada in 1958. When finished it went to Greyhound Lines of Canada and remained in the fleet for a number of years. Greyhound Lines of Canada acquired Moore's and later the Grey Goose Bus Line route from Kenora east in order to have a route between eastern and western Canada. When the Trans-Canada Highway was completed around the Canadian side of Lake Superior in 1960, Greyhound of Canada began bus service.

Les Autobus Deshaies, Ltd of Deschaillons, Quebec, was the first of a number of Quebec bus operators to buy Western Flyer buses. The first Deshaies Western Flyer bus was a Model T-32 acquired in 1947. Five more Western Flyer buses joined the Deshaies fleet between 1948 and 1955. Shown here is the Deshaies P-41 Western Canuck acquired in 1958. It had a Cummins diesel engine. Les Autobus Deshaies was one of Quebec's pioneer bus companies beginning in 1920. The main route was between Levis and Montreal on the south shore of the St. Lawrence River. The company was sold in 1979.

Pontiac Bus Lines, Ltd. began operating on the north side of the Ottawa River in Quebec in 1941. The route began in Ottawa, Ontario, and served Hull, Campbell's Bay, Fort Coulonge and Chapeau in Quebec. The bus pictured, a Western Flyer Canuck Model P41R with a GM 6V 71 engine, was delivered to Pontiac Bus Lines in 1959. A Model 500 Western Flyer Canuck was also reported to be in the Pontiac fleet. In 1966, the company was sold to Yves Seguin. In 1982 the name was changed to Autobus Pontiac and it remained that until Carleton Bus Lines purchased the service.

A Southern Ontario bus company, Burley Bus Lines, Ltd., operated a number of Western Flyer-built buses. This bright green and white P-41 Western Canuck was added to the fleet in 1959. It had a GM 471 engine. Another P-41 was acquired in 1961 and had a GM 6V71 engine. When the Western Canuck 500 was introduced in 1965, Burley Bus Lines bought one. Three years later, Burley added three Model 600 Western Flyer buses. Burley Bus Lines originally started in the Coburg, Ontario, area with school buses, but expanded with route service and a charter business. It also operated bus service in the Guelph and Oshawa area. Charterways took over most of Burley's service in 1969 and 1976.

This Western Flyer Coach Company bus was a Model BT-40 and was sold to Yellowhead Coach Lines of Kamloops, British Columbia, in 1960. It accommodated 24 passengers and had a sizable cargo space at the rear. It had an International 450-horsepower gasoline engine and was the last front-engine gasoline-powered bus built by Western Flyer Coach Company for a bus company. A number of similar front-engine buses went to the Canadian Department of Defense in the 1960s. Yellowhead Coach Line was a subsidiary of BC Lines (1947) Ltd. and operated between Kamloops and Vavenby, British Columbia. In 1964 BC Coach Lines and Yellowhead Coach Lines were acquired by Canadian Coachways.

The cities of Prince George and Prince Rupert, British Columbia, are separated by 724 kilometers (450 miles) over Highway 16. On May 19, 1959, Prince Coach Lines, headquartered in Smithers, British Columbia, started bus service along that route. Although the company had two Standard model Western Flyer buses, Western Canuck buses were used on the route after two were delivered in 1960. One of the Model P-41 Western Flyer Canucks is pictured. These buses had GM 6V-71 diesel engines. Prince Coach Lines added three similar Model P-41 Western Flyer Canucks before selling the company to Canadian Coachways in 1965.

Pictured is a Model BT-41 Western Canuck bus built in April 1961 and acquired by Farwest Bus Lines, Ltd. of the aluminum smelter city of Kitimat, British Columbia. Both the community of Kitimat and Farwest Bus Lines began in the early 1950s. The Model BT-41 had a large cargo space in the rear, and 33 passengers could also be accommodated. Farwest and its subsidiary company, Coastal Bus Lines, continues today providing charter bus service and also contract services in several British Columbia communities.

Sechelt Motor Transit, Ltd. was a pioneer British Columbia bus company beginning in 1919 and incorporating on January 4, 1944. The only Western Flyer bus Sechelt Motor Transit acquired was this Model P-41 Western Canuck in 1960. In 1970, under new ownership, the service became known as SMT Coach Lines, Ltd. Maverick Coach Lines, Ltd. bought the company in January 1981. The route operated was between Vancouver and Powell River.

Autobus Nolin, Inc. of Quebec City, Quebec, had one Western Canuck P-41 bus in its fleet and it is shown here. It was acquired in 1960 and had a GM 6V71 diesel engine. Autobus Nolin began in 1953 and was incorporated two years later. It operated a number of routes to small rural communities.

A Quebec bus operator, Autobus Gauthier, Inc. of Deschambault, was one of Western Flyer's frequent customers in eastern Canada. It operated several routes in the area with one connecting several villages with Quebec City. Eleven Western Flyer buses were purchased, the first being a 1948 Model T-32. Pictured is a 1961 Model P-41, the last Western Flyer bus purchased by Autobus Gauthier. The company was sold in 1966.

Brewster Rocky Mountain Gray Line of Banff, Alberta, added this glass-topped Western Canuck C-33 bus and one other to its fleet in 1962. These two buses had GM 478 gasoline engines. Brewster had purchased Rocky Mountain Motor Transport and kept the combined name for a short time. Brewster Transport had a rich history and had completed 70 years in business in 1962.

Eagle Bus Lines of Winnipeg, Manitoba, had a 1931 start and operated east of Winnipeg to outer suburban and rural areas. The company had a number of Western Flyer Standard buses in its fleet plus one of the four deck-and-a-half models that Western built in 1956. In 1968 Eagle Bus Lines purchased one of the last P-41 Western Canuck buses built and it is pictured here. Eagle had developed a sizable charter business in the Winnipeg area. Beaver Bus Lines, which also operated charter service, purchased Eagle Bus Lines in 1979.

A year before Sunburst Motor Coaches, Ltd. was sold to Canadian Coachways, two 1965 Western Flyer Model P-41 buses were purchased. These two buses were the last in the Western Flyer P-41 series. Sunburst, headquartered in Edmonton, was an early Alberta bus operation beginning in 1931. It had routes from Edmonton serving Chauvin, Cold Lake, and Camrose in Alberta and Macklin and Lloydminster in Saskatchewan. This P-41 Sunburst bus is pictured in front of the new Western Flyer (1964) Coach factory in Winnipeg.

Pictured is an aerial view of the new 35,000 square-foot (3,251 square-meter) factory of Western Flyer Coach (1964) Ltd. in the Fort Garry Industrial Park in Winnipeg, Manitoba. Abraham Thiessen, president of Grey Goose Bus Lines, and his associates acquired the bus manufacturing company in 1963. The company was reorganized by Thiessen and became known as Western Flyer Coach (1964) Ltd. Manitoba Industry Minister Gurney Evans officially opened the new building.

Of all Western Flyer buses built, this one had the most interesting and varied life. It is pictured here as a tourist office in Thompson, Manitoba, in its final days. It is reported that this 1945 bus was built for a jail bus for Headingly, Manitoba. Its most interesting assignment was its role as a rail bus. In 1984 with funding from federal and provincial sources, the rail bus project was launched. The bus had its wheels and tires removed and replaced with steel railroad wheels. It was to operate a 112 km (70-mile) route between Thompson and the villages of Thicket Portage and Pikwitonei. It never succeeded as a rail bus, but it was a successful tourist office for a short time.

The Toronto Transportation Commission needed to replace its trolley bus fleet and in 1968 bids were advertised. Flyer Industries submitted a bid and it was accepted. Bodies for 151 trolley buses designated as Model E700 were involved. Motors for the vehicles were refurbished motors from retired trolley buses. Deliveries for the new trolley buses, one of which is pictured, began in 1972 and the order was completed the next year. No new trolley buses had been built in Canada since 1954.

The Hamilton (Ontario) Street Railways (HSR) had been operating trolley buses since 1950, and in 1971 fleet replacement was considered. The HSR took a look at the Toronto Transportation Commission's Flyer Industries Model E700 trolley buses and followed with an order for 40 of the E700 trolley buses. Delivery took place in 1972-73 and like the trolley buses for Toronto they also had refurbished motors from older trolley buses. Two of the Hamilton Flyer E700 trolley buses are pictured.

Flyer Industries continued to offer trolley buses as one of its products throughout the 1970s. A significant order was received in 1974 from the San Francisco (California) Municipal Railway (Muni). This order, for 343 Model E800 40-foot trolley buses, was the second largest order for trolley buses in the United States and Canada.

The Massachusetts Bay Transportation Authority (MBTA), Boston, Massachusetts, became one of the first transit systems to acquire both trolley buses and diesel buses from Flyer Industries. In 1976, 50 Model E800 trolley buses (below) replaced an older fleet operated by the MBTA. These new trolley buses had a passenger door on the left side to allow in-station transfers to and from subway trains at the Harvard Station in suburban Cambridge. In 1981, 168 Model 901A diesel buses (left) were delivered to the MBTA.

Dayton, Ohio, has had an interesting trolley bus history. Its first trolley bus system began in 1933. At one time there were five companies operating trolley buses in the Dayton area. Consolidation followed and in 1972 the public Miami Valley Regional Transit Authority was established. Three years later, the aging trolley bus fleet was replaced with 64 Model E800 Flyer Industries trolley buses. One of the 1975 Flyer Industries trolley buses is pictured.

This Western Flyer Model T-28/32 is pictured at a rest area on a route of International Transit Limited between Kenora, Ontario, and Fort Frances. The route is very scenic, going through forests and along Lake of the Woods. This Western Flyer was added to International Transit's fleet in 1951. In 1960 Excel Coach Lines of Kenora bought the route and another route between Kenora and Red Lake.

Several bus manufacturers followed the deck-and-a-half design after the Greyhound Scenicruiser was introduced in 1955. Western Flyer Coach was one of these manufacturers and built four deck-and-a-half buses. Pictured is one of the T-36 two-level buses built for Thiessen Transportation, Ltd. of Winnipeg, Manitoba. It is seen leaving the Graham Avenue bus terminal in downtown Winnipeg. Other Winnipeg companies which had the two-level buses were Red River Motor Coach, Moore's Trans-Canada Bus Lines and Eagle Bus Line. The four buses had International 501-horsepower engines.

Moore's Taxi, Ltd., of Winnipeg, Manitoba, had one intercity bus route, known as Moore's Trans-Canada Bus Line between Winnipeg and Kenora, Ontario. Moore's only had a small fleet, but had several Western Flyer models, including this deck-and-a-half model, one of the four built in 1955 and 1956. The Winnipeg-Kenora route was a part of the eventual Trans Canada highway.

Canadian Coachways expanded passenger travel in Northern Alberta and British Columbia, followed by adding destinations in Yukon and Northwest Territories. Canadian Coachways carried package express on all its routes. This became an important part of the service and the volume of package express increased. As a result, a combination bus/truck was developed called a Bruck. The first Bruck, a 1944 Model T-24 Western Flyer, was converted by Western in Winnipeg. There were 13 of these unique vehicles in the Coachways fleet, including this 1951 model destined to Alaska.

Pictured is one of 26 Western Flyer Canuck model buses purchased by Canadian Coachways. Although Coachways acquired other makes of buses, the Western Canucks were the most durable to withstand the rough dusty roads and extreme cold temperatures. The Western Canuck P-37 bus shown here in Edmonton was preparing for the 1,454 km (903 mi.) trip to Yellowknife, the capital of the Northwest Territories.

The first Model 500 Western Flyer Coach bus was built in 1964. It was acquired by Canadian Coachways soon after it was built. The Model 500 pictured carries an Anchorage sign. Canadian Coachways acquired Alaska Motor Coach Co. in 1963 and formed Alaska Coachways. It is doubtful that this Model 500 was ever assigned to Alaska Coachways service.

Attractively posed at a Kenora, Ontario, park is this P-37 Western Canuck of Excel Coach Lines. The Canuck model was introduced by Western Flyer Coach, Ltd. in 1955, and became very popular. Excel Coach Lines was a small bus company beginning in 1933, first providing school bus service and expanding to operate Kenora town service, then taking on intercity service between Kenora and Fort Frances and Kenora and Red Lake. Charter service was also an important part of Excel's business.

In 1964, Western Flyer Coach developed a new model, the Canuck 500. It had large side windows, silversiding, a restroom and other changes from previous models. The Detroit Diesel 6V-71 diesel engine was standard. Only 25 Canuck Model 500 buses were built, and Saskatchewan Transportation Company (STC) bought 13 of them. More than 30 Canuck P-37 and P-41 models were also in the STC fleet. Saskatchewan Transportation Company reportedly had the most Western buses of any commercial bus operator.

The Model 600 Western Flyer was introduced in 1967. A dozen bus companies bought this new bus. Grey Goose Bus Lines of Winnipeg, Manitoba, acquired 10 of the 36 that were reported to have been built. Pictured is one of the 1968 Grey Goose Model 600 buses leaving the Winnipeg Bus Terminal destined to the poetically named city of Deloraine in southwestern Manitoba. The 600 models were powered by Detroit Diesel 8V-71N diesel engines. The Model 600 was 38 feet (11.58 meters) long, longer than the regulated length for buses in most jurisdictions. It could accommodate 45 passengers without a restroom. There was also a Model 600A with a redesigned window arrangement.

The 700 series transit buses were the first large transit buses built by Western Flyer Coach, Ltd. They were introduced in 1967, while the company was still owned by Abraham Thiessen and his associates. On the side of the bus was the message "'Manitoba-growing to beat 70!'" This bus originally was a demonstrator and then leased to Winnipeg Transit. It was later purchased, renumbered and painted the Winnipeg Transit orange and cream.

New Flyer Industries introduced the first full-sized low-floor transit bus, the Model D40LF, to the United States and Canadian markets in 1991. The first D40LF bus was delivered to the Port Authority of New York and New Jersey for shuttle service between airport terminals. This new model was well received. The bus industry had been using wheelchair lifts exclusively on the larger buses. The lifts required considerable maintenance and were time consuming when activated. Low-floor buses also contributed to faster service by cutting dwell time at stops.

The Chicago Transit Authority (CTA) has had a number of New Flyer buses in its fleet. It placed an order for 199 Model D900A buses in 1983. The buses had a light-and-dark-green livery when they were first delivered. The green color had been a tradition for Chicago buses for more than 50 years. In 1987, the CTA decided on a new livery, which was predominately white with red and blue trim.

In 1994, the Chicago Transit Authority (CTA) ordered 65 New Flyer D40LF buses, one of which is shown here. Three of these buses were hydrogen powered. In 2005, the CTA contracted with New Flyer for 688 40-foot models. Most of these were low emission diesel buses, however, 20 were diesel-electric hybrid models. CTA has continued to add New Flyer buses under an option which includes 150 Model DE60LF articulated buses.

Orange County (California) Transit Authority (OCTA) has had New Flyer buses in its fleet almost 20 years. In 1990, 53 Model D40HF buses were acquired. In 1996, 117 New Flyer Model D40LF buses were added. Two of these are diesel hybrid buses and one is pictured. There are also two gasoline hybrid buses in the fleet. An order for 299 Model C40LF compressed natural gas buses are the latest to arrive at OCTA from New Flyer Industries. Thirty of these buses have Express bus seating configuration and 92 are for Bus Rapid Transit service. OCTA has an active fleet of 575 buses, a majority of which are New Flyer buses.

Pictured are two of the 164 New Flyer Model C40LF buses that went into service for the Washington (D.C.) Metropolitan Area Transit Authority (WMATA) in 2002. The bus at the upper left is pictured at Franklin Square and the lower picture shows one of the buses at Washington's Union Station. The 2002 order from WMATA for New Flyer buses was followed with almost 200 more 40-foot buses. Some were compressed natural gas powered models similar to the buses pictured and others were diesel hybrid models. WMATA announced in 2003 an order for 452 New Flyer buses that are now being delivered. There is an option for 500 additional buses from New Flyer. This was later amended to 950 options. To date, this is the largest order of hybrid buses in the world.

Winnipeg (Manitoba) Transit took delivery of 10 Model D40i Invero New Flyer buses in 2004. These buses were among the first Winnipeg buses to have a new overall white livery with multi-color stripes below the windows. Only a limited number of the New Flyer Invero model were built.

This New Flyer Model D40LFR bus was one of the buses in a 33 bus order by Winnipeg (Manitoba) Transit in 2008. This new model was the first order for the Winnipeg fleet to come equipped with air conditioning. Winnipeg Transit has been a Flyer Industries or New Flyer Industries customer since the 1970s.

In 2003, King County Metro, Seattle, Washington, awarded an order for 213 hybrid New Flyer Model DE60LF buses. This was the largest delivery for hybrid buses at that time. King County Metro exercised an option for more of the Model DE60LF hybrid buses which were delivered in 2008. When all the options for additional New Flyer hybrid buses have been delivered, King County Metro is expected to have one of the largest hybrid bus fleets in the world. King County Metro and predecessor Seattle area transit systems have had Flyer or New Flyer buses in their fleets for more than 30 years.

The first articulated trolley buses to operate in Canada began service in Vancouver, British Columbia, in 2007. One is pictured here on a route through Vancouver's Chinatown. The new trolley buses were in an order for 40 New Flyer E60LFR vehicles. Following the initial order, 20 additional Model E60LFR New Flyer trolley buses have been added to the Vancouver fleet. *Photo Lucy MacDonald*

Early in 2007, the Lane Transit District in Eugene, Oregon, opened a new four-mile (6.4 km) busway, most of which is on a dedicated bus roadway. Vehicles for this Bus Rapid Transit (BRT) are six special design articulated New Flyer buses. The buses, which are pictured here at various BRT locations, have doors on both sides to allow the buses to use single stations in the center of the busway. Hybrid diesel-electric power is used for the buses.

In 1994, New Flyer Industries received an order for 60 articulated trolley buses from the San Francisco Municipal Railway (Muni). These trolley buses designated as Model E60HF were the first articulated trolley buses built by New Flyer and the first to be in service in San Francisco, indeed, in all of North America. They joined the 343 two-axle trolley buses purchased by Muni in 1976, resulting in an exclusive Flyer Industries/New Flyer trolley bus fleet in San Francisco.

In 1976, 50 Model E800 Flyer Industries trolley buses were delivered to the BC Hydro & Power Authority, operator of transit service in Vancouver, British Columbia, at that time. Pictured at Vancouver's Stanley Park is a Flyer Industries Model E900A trolley bus. It was one of 200 trolley buses which replaced older trolley buses in the BC Transit fleet in 1982. Vancouver has had the largest trolley bus fleet in Canada. Trolley bus service in Vancouver began in 1947. *Photo Alex Regiec*

In 2005, Vancouver, British Columbia, began replacing 244 older Flyer Industries trolley buses with new Model E40LF New Flyer low-floor trolley buses with an attractive modern design. An order for 40 Model E60LF low-floor articulated New Flyer trolley buses followed with deliveries beginning in 2007. *Photo Lucy MacDonald*

In 1978, Flyer Industries introduced the Model D901 series of transit buses. The front of the bus received some changes, but the body was similar to the Model 800 series. Metro Transit of Seattle (now King County Metro) took delivery of 224 Model D901 40-foot and 36 Model D901 35-foot buses between 1979 and 1981. The Model D901 buses were among the first sold by Flyer Industries to any transit system, and this was the first large order to a transit system in the United States. Since then many New Flyer buses have entered the bus fleet in the Seattle area.

The Municipality of Anchorage, Alaska, organized a system to operate buses within the Anchorage area in 1974. Among the first full-sized buses acquired new were 18 Model D901, 40-foot buses from Flyer Industries in Winnipeg, Manitoba. As the system expanded, Anchorage added 18 New Flyer D40LF buses. There was concern that low-floor buses might not be right for winters in Alaska, but the buses managed to perform very well.

Mississauga (Ontario) Transit was one of a number of new bus transit systems that emerged as a result of the growth of the Metropolitan Toronto suburban area. Mississauga Transit had its beginning in 1974 and began developing a sizable bus fleet. In 1976, this Model D800A Flyer Industries bus and nine others were acquired. Buses from New Flyer Industries were added in following years. Mississauga Transit featured all-white buses with interesting orange graphics.

This attractive two-toned blue Flyer Model D901A bus joined the Calgary (Alberta) Transit fleet with nine others in December 1982. Calgary Transit became a Flyer customer in 1972 when 22 Model D700A buses were acquired. A similar number of Model D800 Flyer buses followed. In the 1990s when New Flyer low-floor buses were built, Calgary began equipping their fleet with the new low-floor models.

The people of Toronto, Ontario, began seeing Model 901 Flyer Industries buses on the city's streets in 1985. Almost 200 of these buses, one of which is pictured here, became a part of the 1,463-bus fleet operated by the Toronto Transit Commission (TTC). Ten years earlier the TTC acquired 153 trolley buses built by Flyer Industries. In addition to the buses and trolley buses, TTC also had 146 light rail vehicles, 109 PCC street cars and 630 subway cars in the 1980s.

Pictured with the impressive Detroit Renaissance Center in the background is one of the 124 New Flyer Model D40HF buses acquired in 1993 by the Detroit Department of Transportation. In 2004, 196 New Flyer Model D40LF buses were purchased. The Detroit Department of Transportation is one of the oldest municipal transportation organizations in the United States. It began in 1922.

Pictured is one of the 75 New Flyer D40HF buses that entered Buffalo, New York's Niagara Frontier Transportation Authority's (NFTA) bus fleet in 1993. In addition to urban service in Buffalo, the NFTA serves Niagara Falls and a number of other communities in the area. It was established in 1974.

Passing in front of the Paris Casino in Las Vegas is one of the 90 New Flyer D40HF buses acquired by the Citizens Area Transit (CAT) in Las Vegas in 1992. Las Vegas was the last large city in the United States to form a public transit system. American Transit Corporation (now Veolia Transportation) was the management company chosen to manage and operate the new system. By 1994, CAT began acquiring New Flyer low-floor buses and articulated New Flyer buses, both Model D60HF and D60LF models. The Paris Casino featured behind the bus on Las Vegas Boulevard is one of the many spectacular casinos in Las Vegas. It features a replica of the Eiffel Tower and other Paris landmarks.

The Metropolitan Transit Commission (MTC) serving the Minneapolis-St. Paul, Minnesota, area has more than 100 New Flyer articulated buses in service. In 1998, this Model D60HF New Flyer bus and 54 others were acquired. The first order for the New Flyer articulated buses came in 1991. The MTC originated in 1969, replacing the private Twin City Rapid Transit Company.

New York Transit Authority (NYCTA) began ordering buses from New Flyer Industries in 1997. That year, 70 Model D60HF bused were delivered. The next year 40 more Model D60HF New Flyer buses were purchased. In 2000, the order for the New Flyer D60HF buses increased to 200 units and in 2003, another 260 were added to the NYCTA fleet. One of the buses in that order is pictured. *Photo Alex Regiec*

The Government of Ontario began providing commuter rail service in the Toronto, Ontario, area in 1967. It was known as GO Transit. The bus fleet grew from the 1970s to today's fleet of about 300 buses, most of which are intercity type. In 1991, GO Transit purchased 50 one-door suburban buses from New Flyer Industries. Pictured here is one of these Model D40HF buses shown ready to leave the New Flyer factory in Crookston, Minnesota.

Beaver Bus Lines, Winnipeg, Manitoba, purchased this 1994 New Flyer Model D40HF demonstrator bus in 1999. It is pictured on Winnipeg's Portage Avenue operating on the Winnipeg-Selkirk service. Beaver Bus Lines is the only bus operator to have purchased both Western Flyer and New Flyer buses. The Beaver Bus Lines Western Flyer bus is pictured on page 30.

The second order for the newly introduced New Flyer low-floor buses went to BC Transit, Victoria, British Columbia. Ten of the Model D40LF New Flyer buses, one of which is pictured, began service in Victoria in 1992. BC Transit is responsible for urban and regional transit in almost 50 locations throughout British Columbia, and New Flyer buses have been operating in a number of locations.

West Vancouver Municipal Bus Line in British Columbia traces its rich history back to 1913. It is said to be the oldest municipal bus operation still serving. Pictured is one of the most recent buses in the West Vancouver Municipal Bus Line fleet. It is a 1995 New Flyer Model D40LF low-floor bus, one of several in today's fleet. Although associated with BC Transit, this bus carries a distinctive dark blue livery.

Edmonton (Alberta) Transit began using low-floor buses in 1998 when 80 New Flyer D40LF buses were purchased. The following year 48 more Model D40LF New Flyer buses were added. New Flyer buses were not new to Edmonton. Model D800 buses were acquired in 1974, and Model D800B buses entered the Edmonton fleet in 1977.

Transit service by the City of Calgary, Alberta, has just celebrated its 100th anniversary. When the city began transit service in the first decade of the 20th century, Calgary was experiencing a 961 percent increase in population, from less than 5,000 to more than 40,000. Now Calgary's population is more than one million. Pictured is one of the 50 New Flyer Model D40LF buses delivered in 2001 to Calgary Transit. The first low-floor New Flyer buses went into service in Calgary in 1992. Calgary Transit has had Flyer Industries or New Flyer buses in its fleet since 1971.

This New Flyer D40LF bus was purchased by the City of Regina, Saskatchewan, for its transit system. The picture shows one of the 1997 buses at a layover stop at the University of Regina transit terminal. *Photo Alex Regiec*

Saskatoon (Saskatchewan) Transit added the first Flyer Industries buses to its fleet in 1976 when 10 Model D800 buses were delivered. The following year 25 Model D800B buses were added. The newest New Flyer buses being added to the Saskatoon Transit fleet are Model DE40LFR buses, one pictured at the University of Saskatchewan. Saskatoon Transit recently introduced a Bus Rapid Transit service known as the DART and it was operating in that service. *Photo Paul Bateson*

Metro Transit in Halifax, Nova Scotia, has been operating a large fleet of New Flyer buses for a number of years. Pictured in the foreground is a 2006 Model D40LF bus. The other bus is a New Flyer D40LF delivered in 2005. The Metro Transit 2005 models operate a Metrolink service in the Halifax metropolitan area. These buses have special graphics, air conditioning, and deluxe appointments. The Halifax skyline is in the background of this view.

The New Flyer Invero model bus was introduced in 2001. It was a special low floor "premium" design bus model. Several transit properties acquired Invero buses. The London (Ontario) Transit Commission ordered 36 of the Invero buses in 2002.

Pictured is one of the newest buses of the Hamilton (Ontario) Street Railway Company (HSR). This New Flyer Model DE60LFR bus and six others were acquired in 2007. They are operating a special express bus service through Hamilton branded as the B-Line. The buses have diesel hybrid drive systems. The HSR has a rich history of municipally operated transit since 1875, with horse cars and sleighs in the early days, then street cars, trolley buses and now an all-bus fleet.

The Ottawa-Carleton (Ontario) Regional Transit Commission (OC Transpo) services include exclusive busways called Transitways. They were established in 1987 and have expanded since. Pictured at one of the Transitway stations in Ottawa is one of the 170 2001-2002 New Flyer Model D60LF low floor buses used on the Transitways. One important advantage of the Transitways is that the buses can leave the Transitway and serve neighborhoods on normal streets. *Photo Paul Bateson*

Brampton, located in the Greater Toronto area, has experienced rapid growth in recent years. Brampton Transit was established in 1974 with a small fleet of buses and now has a fleet of more than 250 buses. Five Flyer Model D800B-9635 were purchased in 1978 and three New Flyer Model D40HF buses were added in 1996. A total of 73 New Flyer Model D40LF buses began entering the Brampton Transit fleet in 2002 with an order for 31 buses followed by 17 in 2003 and 35 in 2004. The first of these acquisitions, bus number 0201, is pictured at the Bramalea Transit Centre. *Photo Paul Bateson*

Oakville (Ontario) Transit is one of the many suburban communities in the Southern Ontario area that established a transit system in the early 1970s. There was a need for transportation in the area and the system has expanded as the population has grown. Pictured is one of the four New Flyer D40LF buses that were acquired by Oakville Transit in 1995.

Pictured in front of the one time transatlantic ocean liner Queen Mary, is one of Long Beach (California) Public Transportation Company's New Flyer Model D40LF buses. In 1995, Long Beach placed its first order for New Flyer buses. In following years more of the Model D40LF buses were purchased, along with 13 Model D60LF articulated buses.

Alternate fuel buses were introduced by New Flyer Industries in 1994. The compressed natural gas (CNG) Model C40LF pictured is one of 45 buses delivered to Omnitrans of San Bernardino, California, in 2000. Omnitrans, which serves a large area, began in 1976. It has more than 100 New Flyer CNG buses in operation. Omnitrans has also been operating several New Flyer gasoline-electric hybrid buses.

Community Transit is the name of the bus system that was formed in 1976 to serve the fast-growing communities of Snohomish County north of Seattle, Washington. Among the first buses acquired by the system were 24 Model D800B Flyer Industries buses. They were added in 1979. More Flyer Industries buses were added in the following years. In 1995, the first low-floor buses were purchased. They were New Flyer Model D40LF buses. Low-floor articulated buses, also from New Flyer, were added in 1998. Pictured is one of these D60LF Models. From a small beginning 30 years ago, Community Transit now operates more than 300 buses, a majority of which are various New Flyer models.

Pierce County Transit, serving the Tacoma, Washington, area, has a fleet of more than 250 New Flyer buses. Most are Model C40LFR buses like the 2006 New Flyer bus pictured. There are also Model C30LF and C60LF New Flyer buses in service. Pierce County Transit was one of the first transit systems in the United States to use compressed natural gas for the majority of their buses.

New Flyer Industries introduced low-floor articulated buses with the Model D60LF in 1995. The City and County of Honolulu (Hawaii) purchased 45 of the buses in 2000 and 2003. From 2004 to 2007, Honolulu purchased 70 diesel hybrid buses in 40-foot and 60-foot configurations. The extensive bus service on the Island of Oahu has been operated under contract by the Oahu Transit Services since 1991.

Pictured is one of six New Flyer Model D60LF buses acquired by the Spokane (Washington) Transit Authority in 2006. These buses are primarily on a special 15-mile route between downtown Spokane and Eastern Washington University in Cheney, Washington. The buses have fabric seats, parcel racks, and individual reading lights. Free WiFi is available to passengers riding these buses.

Pictured is the first New Flyer low-floor bus to go into service with a transit system in the United States. It was the first bus in a 15-bus order in 1993 by the Champaign-Urbana (Illinois) Mass Transit District which serves the two Illinois cities and the University of Illinois. Additional New Flyer Model D40LF buses have since been added to the District's fleet.

The New Flyer Model D45S was introduced in 1998. It is a 45-passenger intercity coach designed for transit systems with long commuter services. The Metropolitan Transit Authority of Harris County, Houston, Texas, has had 200 of this Model D45S in service. It is also known as the Viking. The New York City Transit Authority acquired three Viking buses in 1999.

Metropolitan Transit Authority of Harris County, Texas, commonly known as Houston Metro, had an initial order of 50 Model D40LF New Flyer buses in 1997, one of which is pictured. Many more have since been added. In addition to diesel buses, Houston also operates New Flyer buses powered by compressed natural gas and liquefied natural gas.

The Metropolitan Atlanta Rapid Transit Authority (MARTA) of Atlanta, Georgia, first acquired New Flyer buses in 1990 when 160 Model D40HF high-floor buses were purchased. In the following years more New Flyer buses were added. In 1996, the first Compressed Natural Gas (CNG) New Flyer Model C40LF low-floor buses were acquired by MARTA. Two of the 178 buses in the order are pictured.

This bus, one of 75 new Model D30LF New Flyer small low-floor buses, was acquired by Capital Metropolitan Transportation Authority, Austin, Texas, in 1997. Also in 1997, Capital Metro bought 70 New Flyer Model D35LF buses. The Capital Metropolitan Transportation Authority began in 1985, replacing Austin Transit Corporation which had operated transit service in Austin for many years.

Columbus, Georgia's METRA Transit System acquired five New Flyer D35LF buses in 1997 and added four more in 2000. One of the Model D35LF buses is pictured at the transit system's transfer station which adjoins the transit system maintenance facility property.

Madison (Wisconsin) Metro purchased 30 New Flyer Model D40LF buses in 2000. One is pictured at one of the modern transfer stations in Madison. At the time, there were approximately 250 buses in service by Madison Metro. There has been a plan to expand the bus service throughout Dane County which would increase the transit coverage and the fleet. Madison is the capital of Wisconsin and also the home of the University of Wisconsin.

The Milwaukee County (Wisconsin) Transit System began buying New Flyer D40LF buses in 1995, adding more each year. At the end of ten years, 470 Model D40LF New Flyer buses had been added to the Milwaukee County fleet, which meant that the majority of the fleet consists of New Flyer buses. Pictured is one of an order of 30 of these buses purchased in 2003.

Janesville (Wisconsin) Transit received nine New Flyer D35LF buses in 2001 and eight more in 2006. These buses provide the basic transit service for the city. An intercity route between Janesville and Beloit is jointly operated by the Janesville and Beloit transit systems. The bus system in Janesville has been a municipally operated system for more than 50 years.

The first New Flyer D35LF bus built and delivered in the 21st Century was this bus for the Rockford (Illinois) Mass Transit District. It was one of nine buses delivered at the time. Today's municipal Rockford system began in 1970, replacing the private Rockford Transit Corporation, a division of the American Transit Corporation.

New Flyer Industries added 35-foot low-floor transit bus models to its production line in 1998. The first of the Model D35LF buses went to Lehigh and Northampton Transportation Authority, Allentown, Pennsylvania, soon after the model was introduced. In 1999, the Erie (Pennsylvania) Metro Transit Authority purchased this Model D35LF New Flyer bus and six others. The next year, Erie added six more. The Erie Transit Authority was formed in 1967.

Centre Area Transportation Authority (CATA) has been operating transit service in State College, Pennsylvania, since 1975 when it replaced private transit service. CATA began acquiring New Flyer buses in 1997. The bus pictured is one of eight New Flyer Model C40LF buses added in 1998. Both 35-foot and 40-foot New Flyer buses are operated. At the present time the entire CATA fleet uses compressed natural gas. Originally, Penn State University, which is located in State College, provided campus bus service, but in 1999 CATA assumed the service. CATA is also involved in a hydrogen powered demonstration project.

The historic city of Charlottesville, Virginia, home of the University of Virginia, has a small transit service, the Charlottesville Transit Service. It has been operating New Flyer D35LF buses since 1998 when ten were acquired. Two more, one of which is pictured, were added to the fleet in 2001. Although Charlottesville Transit Service serves the University of Virginia, there is also a separate campus bus service.

Blacksburg (Virginia) Transit was established in 1983 to serve Blacksburg, neighboring Christiansburg and Virginia Tech University. Blacksburg Transit has a fleet of New Flyer low-floor buses including the Model D40LF pictured. It is one of those delivered in 2007. In addition to 40-foot New Flyer buses, the Blacksburg fleet also has 35-foot and 30-foot New Flyer buses.

The Rochester Genesee (New York) Transportation Authority's Regional Transit Division acquired its first New Flyer buses in 1999 when 33 Model D40LF buses were added to the fleet. One of these buses is pictured in downtown Rochester in 2002. Also in 1999, ten New Flyer Model D60LF articulated buses were purchased for the Rochester service. The Rochester Genesee Transportation Authority was established in 1969. In addition to the Regional Transit Division serving Rochester, there are six other divisions serving individual communities in the area.

The Central Ohio Transit Authority (COTA), Columbus, Ohio, operates more than 75 New Flyer Model D40LF buses. The first group was delivered in 2001 and the second order was added in 2004. One of the buses in the 2004 order is shown. COTA began as a publicly owned system in 1971. Columbus Transit Co. was the previous operator.

Capital Area Transportation Authority (CATA) in Lansing, Michigan, acquired its first ten New Flyer Model D40LF buses in 1996, and 48 more were added in 2001. Model D60LF New Flyer buses were purchased in 2003. In 2007 three of the New Flyer Model DE60LFR buses entered the CATA fleet. One is pictured at the Michigan State University in East Lansing. CATA also operates campus bus service at the university.

Pictured is one of 100 New Flyer Model D40LF buses that went into service for the Southeastern Pennsylvania Transportation Authority (SEPTA), Philadelphia, Pennsylvania, in 2002. This order was followed by additional orders, and by the end of 2005 there were more than 650 New Flyer buses in the SEPTA fleet. Included were 32 Model DE40LF New Flyer diesel-electric hybrid buses.

Philadelphia, Pennsylvania, has the oldest continuously operating trolley bus system in North America. It started in 1923. The latest of a variety of trolley bus types is pictured here. It is one of 38 New Flyer Model E40LFR trolley buses which began replacing older vehicles in 2008. Southeastern Pennsylvania Transportation Authority is the present operator of the trolley bus system in Philadelphia. *Photo Bill MacDonald*

On October 27, 2008, the Euclid Avenue Bus Rapid Transit in Cleveland, Ohio, was dedicated. New Flyer Industries was chosen to build the 20 special state-of-the-art vehicles for the service. Pictured are two of the modern hybrid articulated New Flyer Model DE60LFA buses. The Bus Rapid Transit route runs 9.8 miles along the Euclid Avenue corridor between downtown Cleveland and University Circle. An exclusive roadway is used by the buses. The entire Euclid Avenue project features improvements along the route, including buildings, pedestrian walkways, special landscaping, central island stations, and other improvements. *Photos by Jerry Masek, Greater Cleveland Regional Transit Authority*

The XCELSIOR is the newest New Flyer bus. It was introduced at the American Public Transportation Association exposition in San Diego in October 2008. XCELSIOR has a number of new features including attractive streamlined styling both inside and outside, wider entrance door and ramp, increased seating with more forward facing seats, interior LED lighting, longer lasting LED headlights, all-wheel disc brakes and other changes. It is also lighter weight and produces less noise than previous similar sized buses.

These two sales brochures were the first published by Western Auto and Truck Body Works. They gave specifications, pictures and other information about the post World War II Western Flyer coaches.

The Western Flyer Canuck was publicized in this 1953 brochure, reprinted in part from the *Motor Truck & Coach* magazine in 1953.

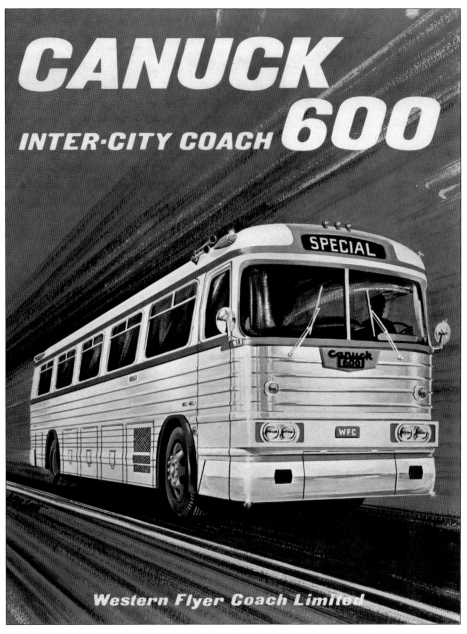

A colorful brochure describing the Western Canuck Model 600 coach. It was distributed in 1964.

The Models D901 and 902 transit buses produced by Flyer Industries were presented in this brochure.

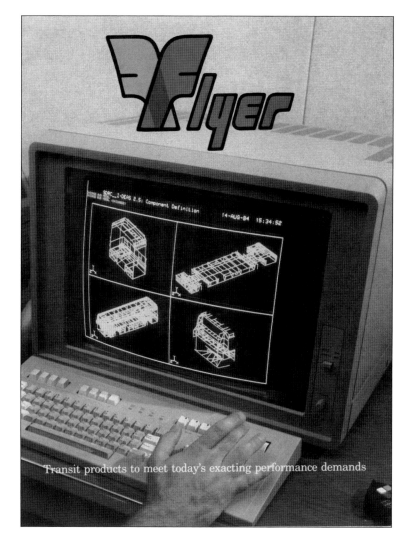

Another brochure of the early 1980s describes the production of the Flyer Industries Model 900 buses and trolley buses.

40 SERIES LOW FLOOR TRANSIT COACH

New Flyer Industries
Driving Innovation

This one-page, full-color piece presented the New Flyer Industries low-floor buses when these buses were first introduced in the early 1990s.

Building Buses

new Flyer

BUILDING BUSES is an in-depth presentation of the steps involved in producing many of the buses built by New Flyer Industries.

MILES AHEAD is one of the recent descriptive booklets produced by New Flyer Industries in the 21st Century.

ABOUT THE AUTHORS

William A. (Bill) Luke began his interest in bus transportation when he was in school in his hometown of Virginia, Minnesota. He had become familiar with the buses of the United States by riding buses, visiting with bus people, and reading articles about bus transportation in various publications.

Bill had some knowledge about Canadian buses, but it wasn't until a visit to the Canadian city of Port Arthur (now Thunder Bay), Ontario, that it was possible to see the Western Flyer buses operated by International Transit Limited. On other Canadian trips, there was the opportunity to see more Western Flyer buses.

After serving in the army in the mid-1940s, one of Bill's goals was to travel to Winnipeg to see more of the Canadian bus industry and possibly visit the Western Flyer factory. He wrote a letter to Western Flyer telling about the Winnipeg visit he planned and asking if a stop to see the Western Flyer factory would be possible. Bill received a letter from John Coval, the Western Flyer president, telling him he would be welcomed at Western Flyer. In September 1947, Bill went to Winnipeg and visited the Western Flyer factory. He met with John Coval and was given a personal tour of the bus building process. He received a number of interesting brochures and pictures.

In 1948, after a move to Minneapolis, Bill became employed by Jefferson Transportation Co. While working in Minneapolis there were opportunities to travel to Winnipeg at least once or twice a year. Each time Bill visited Western Flyer and enjoyed visiting with John Coval and also Bill Dershko. John, who had become a good friend, could be identified by anyone by his felt (straw in the summer) fedora hat and a cigar between the fingers of his left hand. He kept his right hand free to shake hands with his many friends.

Bill's first trip on a Western Flyer bus was between Kenora and Fort Francis, Ontario. It was operated by International Transit. He also rode other Western Flyer, Western Canuck and Western Model 600 buses of Moore's Trans-Canada Bus Line, Red River Motor Coach Line, Saskatchewan Transportation Company and Grey Goose Bus Lines.

Bill Luke stands beside a Western Flyer Model T-32 bus of International Transit, Limited at a rest stop between Kenora and Fort Francis, Ontario, in October 1952.

Linda Metler and Bill Luke stand in front of a New Flyer Model D40LF bus of Spokane (Washington) Transit Authority.

For a number of years, Bill handcrafted small wooden buses and painted them in appropriate company colors. He wanted to make a model Western Canuck but he wanted to match the colors used by Saskatchewan Transportation Company on their buses. Bill wrote John Coval requesting paint chips of the Saskatchewan buses. John responded by sending Bill two small cans of paint of the Saskatchewan colors. Bill then made two models of the Saskatchewan Transportation Co. Canucks and sent one to John, with the exact colors of the livery.

After John Coval sold the company to Abraham Thiessen, Ron Thiessen, his son, became active in the company and Bill established a friendship with Ron. They visited together on numerous occasions. Like John Coval, Ron often provided Bill with brochures, company news and photographs of buses.

Bill and his wife, Adelene, established Friendship Publications and *Bus Ride* magazine after moving to the West in the late 1960s. Contact with Western Flyer continued. Part of Friendship Publications' business was conducting maintenance seminars. Two were held in Winnipeg and each time Flyer Industries gave tours of the factory to attendees.

Jan den Oudsten of Holland acquired Flyer Industries in 1989 and it became New Flyer Industries. When Bill and his wife attended a bus industry exhibition in Holland in 1984, they met Jan den Oudsten. They also visited the Den Oudsten bus-building factory in Woerden, Holland. In addition to touring the factory they met with a number of the Den Oudsten management people.

In recent years, Bill visited New Flyer in Winnipeg and also visited the plants in Crookston and St. Cloud, Minnesota. Bill has established a good friendship with the present New Flyer management people, not only when visiting the factories but also at various bus industry events. Bill has always appreciated the good relationship he has had with Western Flyer, Flyer Industries and New Flyer Industries. Bill and co-author Linda Metler are grateful for all their assistance in making this book possible.

Bill and Adelene Luke owned Friendship Publications for more than 30 years. In addition to *Bus Ride Magazine* the company pub-

Wood model of a Saskatchewan Transportation Company Western Canuck bus that was handcrafted and painted by Bill Luke in 1955.

lished directories and conducted seminars for the bus industry. Bill has traveled extensively and authored or co-authored 12 bus industry books beginning with the *Bus Industry Chronicle* in 2000. Three of the books and this one have been co-authored with Linda Metler. Bill and Adelene live in Spokane, Washington.

Linda Metler began her association with the bus industry as an employee of Friendship Publications. In addition to writing for *Bus Ride* she was graphics manager, helping transition the company to desktop publishing. Linda traveled extensively for the publication, visiting many bus companies and transit agencies in the United States and Canada and writing articles following the visits. Her interest in computers helped in compiling and completing this book. Linda and her husband, Don, also live in Spokane. They have two grown daughters and three grandchildren.

More Great Titles From

Iconografix

All Iconografix books are available from direct mail specialty book dealers and bookstores worldwide, or can be ordered from the publisher. For book trade and distribution information or to add your name to our mailing list and receive a **FREE CATALOG** contact:

Iconografix, Inc.
PO Box 446, Dept BK
Hudson, WI, 54016

Telephone: (715) 381-9755,
(800) 289-3504 (USA),
Fax: (715) 381-9756
info@iconografixinc.com
www.iconografixinc.com

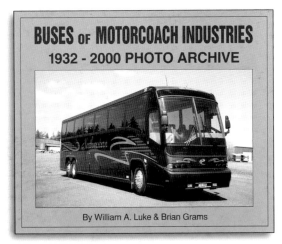
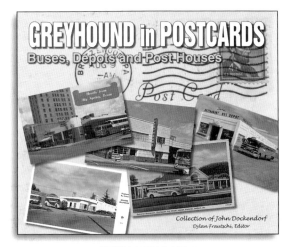
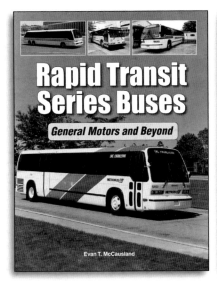
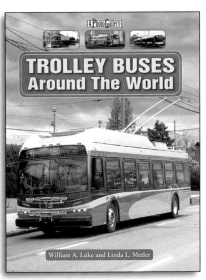
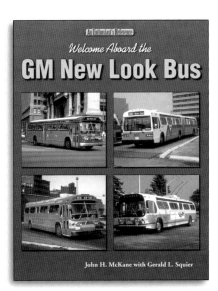
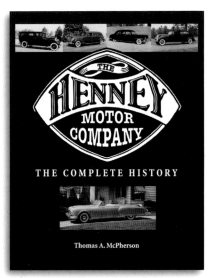